Photo: Sebastian Bourges

Angela Betzien is an award-winning playwright. Her work includes *Dog Wins Lotto* (Queensland Theatre Company, 1997), *Playboy of the Working Class* (Queensland Theatre Company, 2001), *The Suitcase* (RealTV/Stage X Festival, 2001), *Princess of Suburbia* (RealTV, 2001), *Kingswood Kids* (La Boite Theatre, 2002), *The Orphanage Project* (Queensland Theatre Company, 2003), *Children of the Black Skirt* (Queensland Arts Council and RealTV, 2003) *Hoods* (Sydney Opera House:Ed and Regional Arts Victoria, 2006), *Girl Who Cried Wolf* (Arena Theatre, 2008, Windmill Theatre, 2011), *The Dark Room* (Black Swan, 2009) and *The Teenage Alchemist* (Camp Quality, 2009). In 2011 Belvoir will present the NSW premiere of *The Dark Room*. *Children of the Black Skirt* and *Hoods* have been published by Currency Press.

War Crimes

Angela Betzien

CURRENCY PRESS
SYDNEY

CURRENCY TEENAGE SERIES

First published in 2011
by Currency Press Pty Ltd,
PO Box 2287, Strawberry Hills, NSW, 2012, Australia.
enquiries@currency.com.au
www.currency.com.au

Reprinted in 2014

NATIONAL LIBRARY OF AUSTRALIA CIP DATA

Author: Betzien, Angela, 1978–.
Title: War crimes / Angela Betzien.
ISBN: 9780868199184 (pbk.)
Target Audience: For secondary school age.
Subject: War–Drama.
Dewey Number: A822.4.

Set for Currency Press by Dean Nottle.
Cover design by Laura McLean. Cover shows Jada Alberts and Zahra Newman.
Cover photograph by Sebastian Bourges.

Contents

Currency Press acknowledges the Traditional Owners of the Country on which we live and work. We pay our respects to all Aboriginal and Torres Strait Islander Elders, past and present.

That morning you saw me on the beach?
It wasn't what you think.
Just got trashed.
Wasn't what you think.

Director's / Playwright's Note

In 2007, in response to a spate of attacks on war memorials in towns and cities across Australia, a war memorial legislation amendment bill was proposed in parliament, increasing penalties for vandalising, defacing, deliberately damaging or behaving inappropriately around war memorials. These events inflamed debate over the ANZAC legend and sparked a call for a resurgence of pride in this national story.

War Crimes was created in response to this and several other real contemporary Australian events, with the intention of stirring up some big questions about our national history, identity and future. Importantly, it raises the question of what is sacred to us as a nation?

Tragically, twenty-seven young Australian soldiers have been killed in Afghanistan since the beginning of the war declared by the United States in 2001. Figures vary, but one source estimates that 873,344 civilians, including women and children, have been killed in Iraq and Afghanistan since this time. Thousands more have been driven from their homes to seek refuge in other parts of the world, including urban and rural Australia. In Australia, some of our neighbours have experienced the reality of war firsthand. They have fled torture, imprisonment and death on a scale unimaginable to many of us.

It seems there's constant debate about who belongs in this country. Whose home is it? Most of the population, not including Indigenous Australians, have ancestors who were immigrants at some time in the last two hundred or so years. They arrived either by boat or by plane and it's fair to assume that all of them were seeking a place of belonging, a home. This is a human need, a human right.

In the midst of all this global and local conflict, it's vital that we become critical of what's happening in this country and the world, to form opinions about local, national and global events based on a variety of sources, not just the mainstream media. Often it's the voices that we don't hear, such as those of young, poor teenage girls, that can be the most insightful.

War Crimes will have its premiere regional schools tour with Arts2GO in August 2011. We're thrilled to be taking this story to young people living in regional Australia. The play has been written for an ensemble of five female performers of diverse cultural backgrounds because RealTV wants to make theatre that reflects the faces on our urban and rural streets, theatre that reflects the stories of those with power, and those without.

Every story is important and our common ground has to be the land we inhabit, a land that was the home of a people for thousands of years, a land that is undeniably ancient and sacred.

Leticia Caceres and Angela Betzien
Melbourne, May 2011

Leticia Caceres directed the premiere season of *War Crimes* for Regional Arts Victoria.

First Production

War Crimes was commissioned by Sydney Opera House:Ed and Regional Arts Victoria Arts2GO. It premiered in Victoria on 1 August 2011. At the time of publication, the cast had not been confirmed.

Director, Leticia Caceres
Composer, Pete Goodwin
Designer, Tanja Beer

Acknowledgements

Jodie Le Vesconte, Peta Brady, Jada Alberts, Maria Coviello, Zahra Newman, Amy Horne, Catherine Davies, Matt Cornell, Laura Milke Garner, Peter Matheson, Chris Mead and Playwriting Australia, Theatre Works, Gasworks, Regional Arts Victoria, Emma Cochran, Emily Aitkins, Footscray youth consultation group (Lorika Kadriu, Hannie McBride, William Ewing, Fahim Ahmad, Cat Leonard, Verena Curr, Bryan Davidson Blue, Emily Goddard), Candy Bowers, Sebastian Bourges, Tanja Beer, Naomi Rukavina, Helen Weder, Wahibe Moussa, Sultana Melike, Noel Jordan, Mia Bucholtz, Julian Meyrick, The Australian Writers' Guild and Copyright Agency Limited (CAL), Casey Nicholls and Deer Park Secondary Drama students, Zilla Turner and Carly Leonard from HLA Management.

We'd also like to thank the Year Nine girls of Mooroopna Secondary College (2008).

REALtv is a Melbourne-based company co-founded by writer Angela Betzien and director Leticia Caceres. With their trademark fusion of physical performance, electronic music and new writing, RealTV creates challenging new theatre for a new generation. RealTV's award-winning plays *Children of the Black Skirt* and *Hoods* have toured extensively across Australia. In 2010 *Hoods* toured internationally to DSCHUNGEL WIEN, Vienna, and Cortile – Theater im Hof, Bolzano. In 2011 RealTV will present a national tour of *Random* by Debbie Tucker Green and *War Crimes* by Angela Betzien. Belvoir Theatre will also present Angela Betzien's *The Dark Room*, a RealTV collaboration.

A Note on Process

War Crimes was commissioned by Sydney Opera House:Ed and Regional Arts Victoria Arts2GO with funds from the Richard Wherrett Award for Excellence in Playwriting. The script was also developed in consultation with a diverse group of young people from across Victoria at the Footscray Community Arts Centre in 2009. The play was later developed and showcased at the National Play Festival in February, 2010.

Publication of this title was assisted by the Commonwealth Government through the Australia Council, its arts funding and advisory body.

Characters

Jade, 16
Lara, 15
Rick, 15
Jordan, 15
Ishtar, 16
Samira, Ishtar's mother
Teacher
Lara's Mum
Miss Cutliff
Manager
A chorus of boys (the Kings)
A chorus of men
A chorus of Iraqi women

The play has been conceived for an ensemble of five female actors.
The casting should reflect the cultural diversity of Australia.
All actors play multiple roles.

Setting

A forgotten coastal town.

SCENE

JADE is running through the dawn.

A soundtrack builds—it is a fragmented news report underscored by a war zone.

Voice The Department of Defence... Private Damien Greer... small coastal town... Cummergunja... has been killed... diggers lost... Afghan conflict to twelve...

    JADE runs faster and faster.

    She is running for her life now as the track intensifies in volume and urgency.

    She collapses.

Jade Stop
    stop
    stop
    stop.

    Waves crashing on the beach.

    JADE is unconscious on the sand.

    Another girl, JORDAN, stares at her from further off.

    JADE wakes, but doesn't see JORDAN at first.

    She checks herself, her bloodied lip and bruised thighs.

    She clocks JORDAN.

    She covers herself up.

    What are you lookin' at?

Jordan They gone.

Jade Piss off.

Jordan I seen 'em go.

Jade Piss off psycho.

    JORDAN flares up for a second then backs away and heads off down the beach.

    Darkness.

    Cummergunja.

LARA appears.

What's it mean?

Lara Why ya askin' us?

RICK appears.

Rick Dunno.

Lara It's Abo isn't it?

Rick Ah mah that's racist.

ISHTAR appears.

Ishtar Means home.

Lara Hey how would you know that?

Jade 'Memba Miss Cutcliff taught us?

Lara/Rick Nuh.

Lara Yeah well means home to us Aussies
not them new Habibis.

Rick Yeah. What youse come here for?

Ishtar Because of war.

Lara Nothin' to do with us.

Rick Didn't youse blow our Damo up?

Lara Damo Greer.

Rick got blown up in…?

Ishtar Afghanistan.

Rick last year.

Lara Hey Ishtar ya rellies have anythin' to do with that?

Rick Yeah?

ISHTAR ignores them.

Lara Why ya askin' us all this stuff?
Huh?

Rick Because of all that bad stuff/that happened?

Lara Well we ain't sayin' zip
about it.

Silence.

Jade Once, we was sisters.

LARA scoffs.

Rick Yeah since we was sperm.

Lara Shut ya mouth germ.

Jade We was sisters forever
never to sever.

Rick Not her

He refers to ISHTAR.

me 'n' Jade 'n' Lara.

Jade We was like Siamese twins
or somethin'.

Rick Then that bad stuff happened.

Jade Changed everythin'.

Lara Ancient history
not goin' over it.

Rick Yeah/but…

Lara Let's just bury it.
Let's just forget it.

Jade Who made you queen bee?

Lara Me.

Jade I'm gunna tell 'em.

Lara Yeah?

Pause.

Go on big mouth
spit it out.

Pause.

Jade See, no-one in this town battled us.

Lara What about the Kings?

Jade What about 'em?

Rick Jade could take 'em on.

Jade Yeah in a second.

Rick They ever lip us
dismiss us
she promise
she mash 'em up.
She look after us.

Lara Yeah she reckoned.

Rick Show 'em.

*The girls morph into the KINGS, a gang of boys from the town,
barking likes dogs.*

Kings Hey chicks show us ya bits.

Jade What did you say?

King Oh sting man you got the queen bee.

3

Jade Do you want some advice for your sexual inadequacy?

King Is it true you suck lemon
that's why you got sour nips?

Jade Rather suck lemon than your limp stick.

Rick Oh man shouldn't have done that Jade
shouldn't have started that.

Jade Why not?

Rick The Kings is tough.

Jade Nuh, they're just pups playin' rough.

Rick Then all that bad stuff happened.

Jade That night
night that changed everythin'

Lara news hits.

Rick Gunja's on TV.

Lara Newsreader reckons Damo Greer's been blown up by a... what?

Ishtar IED.

Rick What?

Ishtar Improvised Explosive Device.

Rick He grew up here.

Jade Sports captain.

Lara Won us the local premiership.

Rick Every chick wanted to do him.

Lara We knew him.

Jade Bull.

Lara True.

Jade Not you.

Pause.

Lara Remember she fainted at the funeral?

Rick Who?

Lara Damo's mum.

Jade He was her only son.
Jus' turned twenty-one.

Rick Hardly got to have any fun.

Silence.

Lara So Ishtar, I asked ya.
Did ya rellies have anything to do with it?

ISHTAR ignores her.

4

Ishtar here thinks she's better than us.
That thing she wears round her head.
Ishtar It's called a hijab.
Lara She stole our Finn.
Rick Coolest boy in our school.
Best surfer in the state.
Lara Ishtar was doin' him. Tried to make out we was all mutts.
Rick Yeah when she's the one/got…
Jade Anyway that night
right
there's somethin' in the air.
Feels dangerous
Rick yeah
Lara/Jade/Rick 'cos Damo's dead
Rick 'n' we got terrorists livin' here.
Lara They're cuttin' shifts at the meatworks.
Reffos robbin' our jobs.
Rick Lara's mum lost her job.
Lara Shut ya gob.

Pause.

So town goes rank.
Soldiers out the army base
hit the town to get tanked.
And Jade…
Jade's all geared up.
Jade Wait up.
Lara Wassup?
Jade Thought you weren't sharin' with us?
Lara Not havin' youse makin' stuff up.
Jade Righto.
Have a go.
Lara There's only one nightclub in this town yeah.
Rick Nah there's the RSL.
Lara S'not a club yo.
Rick Yeah says so.
Lara What?
Rick On the sign it says
Return Services Leagues Club.

Lara That's for old farts not us.

Rick Yeah true no place for hot B girls like me
who need to dance some funky def beats or I'll destruct
I'll erupt.

Lara Ya gunna interrupt?

Rick Nup.

Lara There's only one nightclub in this town.

Rick But it's not like clubs in the city.

Lara How would you know?

Rick I been.

Jade/Lara In your cream-filled dreams.

Jade Anyway we're underage
but we had our ways.

Lara We hang round the door long enough.

Jade Bouncer just actin' tough.

Rick Jade was the magician.

Jade I always got us in.

Lara So Jade's all g'd up.

Jade Yeah right on what?

Lara Dunno some fit.
Ya weren't sharin' with us.

Rick That's shit.

Jade As if...
I was just pissed.

Lara Then they walked in.

Rick Who?

The girls morph into off-duty soldiers.

Jade Army base.
Dunno their names
shaved heads all look the same.

The MEN clock JADE dancing alone and zone in.

The MEN speak in unison.

Men Hey Star what are you drinkin'?

Jade Beam and Coke.

Men We'll keep 'em comin'
if you dance with us.

Jade All four of youse?

Men Reckon you can handle us?

Jade I can take youse all on.

Men Yeah?

Jade In a second.

Lara So Jade geared up a notch
　　showed off
　　kickboxes a pint
　　this height.

Rick I never saw that.

Lara That's 'cos you hurled
　　your pink sick on the floor.

Rick Oh sore.

Lara And with that deadly kick
　　Jade scored an all-night all-you-can-spew card.

Rick Sick.

Lara Yeah real clever trick.
　　So three a.m. the place goes off.
　　Whole club's sinkin' drinks
　　for Damo Greer.
　　Soldiers are singin' war songs
　　and swimmin' in beer
　　'cos Damo's the town hero
　　and he's comin' home in bits tomorrow.

Rick Oh yeah 'n' then you got the shits
　　'cos them soldiers weren't lookin' at you.

Lara Wrong again Rick
　　dipstick.
　　Pretty clear that party
　　was gunna get all nasty
　　so we left.

Rick We tell Jade that?

Lara Nah she was out of it.

Rick Should we have done that?

Lara Jade's a big girl
　　she's tough.

Rick Still…

Lara Okay finish.
　　Don't go thinkin' I'm guilty or nuff
　　'cos I isn't.

JADE dances, the four MEN circling her.

The soundtrack morphs into a war zone.

JADE is engulfed in darkness.

The war track morphs into the thunder of waves on a beach.

SCENE

Morning.

The high school gates.

JADE, earphones in, listens to a score of music and radio fragments.

Voice Twelfth Australian soldier… arrived home this morning… mortal remains… ceremony at the RAAF base… Cummergunja.

> *SAMIRA, an Iraqi woman wearing hijab, enters with her daughter, ISHTAR.*
>
> *SAMIRA speaks with the Iraqi dialect of Arabic.*

Samira Ishtar is that your teacher?

Ishtar Where?

Yeah, that's my teacher.

Samira She is very young.

Ishtar She's not that young.

Samira When I was a teacher/

Ishtar You were a teacher in Iraq Oummi it's different here.

Samira Speak to me in Arabic Ishtar.

Ishtar No.

I'm trying to teach you English.

> *SAMIRA speaks in English.*

Samira Work hard today.

You listen to your teachers.

Ishtar I always do.

Samira Or you wear this all your life.

> *She takes a plastic factory worker's cap from her bag.*

You like it?

Ishtar No.

Samira No?

Ishtar No, I don't want to stink of meat.

> *Silence.*

8

Samira You think I like this work?

Ishtar The bell's about to ring.

Samira I do this for you.

Ishtar I know.

A school bell/factory horn blares.

As ISHTAR leaves, LARA and RICK are passing by.

Rick Hey Ishtar how's Finn?

Lara Yeah you still doin' him?

LARA and RICK spot JADE.

Rick Jade where you been?

JADE pulls her earphones out.

Jade What?

Rick Where you been?

Jade Here 'n' there
runnin'.

Lara You been waggin' for a week.

Rick We was worried.

Jade Youse never called.

Lara Yeah we did Jade we texted ya.
Didn't ya get it?

Jade Nuh.

Lara Ya phone must be broke.

Jade Yeah sure.
You never come visit.

Rick We thought you was shitty with us.

Jade Yeah?
Why would I be shitty with yas?

Rick 'Cos we left ya at the club.

Jade Yeah ya did.

Rick Yeah well I hadda go before me dad finished his shift.

Lara And I hadda go with her to get a lift
told ya before we left.

Jade Nah yas didn't.
I'm on the floor
look around
youse are gone.
Never said nothin' did ya?

9

Rick Sorry/Jade.
Jade Nah.
Rick Do ya hate us?
    Do ya hate our guts?
Jade Hate me sisters?

      Pause.

  Never.
Lara What happened to them jocks you was with?
Jade Huh?
Rick Them army blokes you was dancin' with?
Jade Nothin'.
    I got ripped
    then pissed off.
Lara That's the way
    hey that's our Jade.
    Sorry babe.
Jade Go again on the weekend hey?
Rick What happened to your lip?
Jade Runnin' 'n' I slipped.

SCENE

Day.

A classroom.

Lara We're in class right?
Jade Maths.
Rick Biology isn't it?
Lara Chemistry.
Ishtar History.
Rick It's a mystery.
Lara Whatever it is
    we're not listenin'.
Rick We got Jade's iPod in.
    Stolen last week.
Jade Dick Smith store.
All Score.
Rick Jade's a magician.
Lara So we're sharin'

drownin' out Mr Davidson's borin' lesson
with Missy Elliot's crumpin' rhythm
when alarm goes off.

All   Bomb scare.

Lara   Teacher panics
screams.

Teacher   Single file.
Leave your gear.

All   I ain't goin' nowhere without my stuff.

Rick   What if the bomb is out here Miss?

Lara   Shouldn't we jus' go home 'n' wait for the all clear?

Rick   We helpfully suggest.

Jade   Falls on deaf ears.

Lara   Rumour has it
someone sent a text message.

All   Yo muthas dis is a bomb thret.

Rick   Yeah principal farted at her desk.

All   It's hot out here.

Rick   Haven't they caught the terrorist yet?

ISHTAR appears.

Lara   Just arrest her sir.
[*To ISHTAR*] Where you from again?

Rick   She's Iraqian
or somethin'.

Lara   Aren't we at war with them?

Rick   Yeah didn't they blow our Damo up?

Lara   You got any bombs under ya school uniform?

Ishtar   Yeah take a look.

ISHTAR yanks up her jumper.

Rick   Yo peeps she's gunna blow.

ISHTAR flicks a finger at the girls.

LARA gestures back.

Jade   There's that foster kid
Jordan.

JORDAN is lingering on the outskirts, wearing a dark hood.

JADE eyeballs JORDAN.

Rick Where?

Jade Over there.

   What's her story?

Lara Who cares?

Jade Bell blares.

   Announcement.

Teacher This is the end of the bomb scare.

   Resume your lessons.

All Yeah yeah yeah.

Lara So we're back in…

Ishtar Modern History.

Lara Learning about…

Ishtar The ANZAC mythology.

Jade Teacher asks us what we think is sacred.

Lara I say my pussy.

   He say

Teacher why's that?

Rick He thinks she means her cat.

Lara 'Cos you can't touch this.

   Gold star.

Rick Class goes rah.

Teacher Sacred: worthy of or regarded with religious veneration

   worship or respect.

   Not to be challenged or disrespected.

Lara Hey that's me.

   That's my whole body.

Teacher What do you think this is?

Lara Teacher got a glass jar off his desk.

Rick Sand.

Teacher Where's it from?

Rick Beach.

Teacher Yes correct.

   A very important beach

   a long way from here.

Rick Gold Coast.

Teacher Further than that.

Rick Cairns.

Teacher Think further afield.

Silence.

Come on.
This sand is sacred.
Australians have a sacred connection to this beach.

Rick Cronulla.

Teacher Ishtar?

Ishtar Gallipoli.

Teacher Thank you.

Ishtar We studied this last year.

Rick Looks like a crappy beach sir.
Can you surf there?

Teacher This sand is soaked with the blood
of our soldiers.
Pass it round.
In light of the tragic death of local boy
Private Damien Greer
whom I taught in Grade Eight by the way
I want you all to reflect on the meaning of Gallipoli to you
as a young Australian.

Rick Sir if you did a forensic test
would there really be blood in this sand?

Teacher No Ricky.

Lara Then Reffo gobs up.

Ishtar How were they heroes?

Silence.

Weren't they invading another country?

Rick Hey is she dissin' our diggers?

Teacher It's a bit more complicated than that.

Ishtar How?

Teacher I think you'll find the Turkish were doing some pretty
nasty things to the Armenians at the time.

Ishtar And that's why Australia was invading was it?
To free the Armenians from the Muslims?

Lara Yeah she is.
Hey those diggers died for us.

Teacher Look that's a very good point Ishtar.
Why don't we turn to page thirty-three for some context.

LARA addresses the audience.

Lara See she was dissin' our Damo.

Jade Was not.

Lara Damo died for us.

Rick Yeah to save us from terrorists.

> *Back to the classroom, LARA addresses ISHTAR.*

Lara Why don't you go home?
  Why don't ya jus piss off if ya hate us so much?

> *ISHTAR leaves the class suddenly sick.*
> *Only JADE clocks this.*

SCENE

A cave in the cliffs above the beach.
JADE enters the cave breathless, she's been running.
She finds JORDAN camped there.

Jade Hey.

> *JORDAN wakes up.*

  Are you sleepin' here?

> *JORDAN doesn't move.*

  Can't come here ya know
  not just anyone.

> *No response.*

  Deaf retard?

> *JORDAN stands.*
> *JADE steps back.*

  Wasn't what you think.

> *No response from JORDAN.*

  That morning on the beach you saw me?
  Jus' got trashed.
  Wasn't what ya think
  so don't go spreadin' it.

> *JORDAN is gone.*

  And don't tell anyone about this place.
  That's a warning.

*JADE grabs the rest of JORDAN's belongings and chucks them
out of the cave.*

Take ya crap with ya.

SCENE

Lara Later that night Jade sends us a texty.
Rick Not me.
Lara That's 'cos you don't got no moby.
Jade Public toilet block
ten o'clock.
Lara So we rock up.
Jade's got a can in her hand.
Rick She's graffin' up the walls of the toilet door with stuff.
Lara Jade wassup?
Jade Let's gear up.
Rick And do what?
Jade Jus' muck up.
'Memba last time we did that?
Grade Nine?
Rick Yeah we was blind.
Lara You made that bomb threat didn't ya?
Jade Yo muthas dis is a bom thret.
Lara How come you never told us you was doin' it?
Jade Didn't think jus' did it
like last minute.
Lara Should've told us.
Rick Jade you'll get expelled for that.
Jade So what?
Lara What's this all of a sudden?
Jade They mess with us
we get 'em back.
Rick Yeah.
Who?
Jade All of 'em
whole town.
Rick What's the town done to us?
Jade Everyone's always givin' us shit
do that, do this.
Think about it?

Rick Yeah true.

Jade So youse up for it or not?

Lara We're sisters aren't we?

Jade Then bring it on.

Rick Where we goin'?

Jade Primary school.

Rick Cool.

SCENE

Night.

ISHTAR is running toward the beach.

JORDAN is trudging towards the cliffs.

The girls are running through the back streets of town.

They pass each other in the darkness.

SCENE

The primary school.

The girls are trying to break in through a window.

Rick I ain't been back here since Year Seven.

Jade 'Memba Miss Cutcliff?

Lara Miss Cutcliff was a sour witch.

Jade Sucked under she's bald.

Rick Is she bald?

Lara Lost all her hair 'cos of us.

Jade 'Cos of stress.

Lara We was so bad-arse.

Jade Couldn't handle us.

Lara Thought ya liked her.

Jade Nuh.

Lara Yeah thought ya did hey?
Gave her that teacup on break-up day.

Jade Nuh.

Lara She reckoned you was a good writer.
Wrote a poem for her didn't ya?

Jade Not me
prob'ly Ricky.

Rick Did not.

Lara Jade was in love with her.

Rick Yuk.

Jade Piss off.

> *JADE goes for LARA.*

Lara Jus messin' with ya.

> *The girls crawl through the window, they're inside.*

> *They check out the classroom.*

> *JADE grabs the spray can from her backpack and writes 'Miz Cutcliff is a bald bitch'.*

> *The girls stare in silence.*

Jade Miz Cutcliff was full of it.
Said we could do whatever we wished
just had to believe it.
Somewhere over the rainbow
wish upon a star.
She was a liar.

Lara Then Jade picks up this big jug of PVC glue
slowly unscrews the lid
and pours it all over the carpet.

Rick Then we all weigh in.

Lara It was like a trance we was in

Rick like we was high on somethin'

Lara till we're wasted

Rick till we're pasted
on the classroom floor

Lara can do no more.

Rick And it's real quiet
real relaxed.

Lara Then Jade gets up.

Jade Hey wassup?

Lara/Rick We both seen this look.

> *JADE takes off.*

Jade wait up.

> *JADE is running.*

Jade Cold air

black
pavement cracks
vault the train tracks
split second stumble on gravel
hit grass
startle pass sleeping cows
heads hung low
sudden stampede rapid reverse
third gear
traverse the dry field
quick reflex
side step
sheep's skull dead crow kangaroo cull
catapult cattle grid
hopscotch buttercups
bound barbed wire fence
knees wobble 'n' drop
pause for a split second then
pop
hit the highway bitumen
pitch black
heel toe
toe heel
rip it up
fuck truck
switch
belly-flop the dry ditch
lay low till it goes
then
snap back make tracks
three k from town
dogs bark bird carks
veer north still dark
parked car phone box garbage bins
pain kicks in
muscles twitch
lungs split
drought throat
cough

gob up 'n' spit
focus
count fence posts
one two
Men You want us don't you?
Jade three four
Men Hey Star you want more?
Jade five six
Men Wanna lift?
Jade seven eight
Men I got her she's right mate.
Jade nine ten
Men Let's go then.
Jade last stretch to sea
sprint it
slay it
erase it
sand bluff cloud squall salt wind rock wall
fall
heart hops
pulse drops
stop
stop
stop
stop.

JADE lies exhausted on the beach.

ISHTAR appears in hijab. She watches JADE for a moment then hurries away.

SCENE

The cave.

JADE runs in. She discovers JORDAN camped there.

Jade Told ya not to come here.
Jordan Own it do ya?
Jade Was here first.
Jordan Reckon?
Jade Yeah.
Don't ya have some home to go to?

Jordan Don't you?

Silence.

Jade Everyone at school reckons you're psycho.
Stabbed a girl once didn't ya?
Pencil right through her hand.
Why'd you do that?

Jordan She looked at me.
Stabbed her 'cos she looked at me.

Jade S'posed to be scared by that?

JORDAN spits.

You can't sleep here right.

Jordan What's stoppin' me?

Jade It's sacred this place.
Aboriginal people used to camp here
for thousands of years.
This was their home.

Jordan Yeah well it's mine now.

Jade You can't just trash it
leave ya crap everywhere.

Jordan You me mum now?

Jade Gotta look after it.

Jordan What you black or somethin'?

Jade Might be.

Jordan Don't look it.

Jade What are you?

Jordan I'm nothin'.

Silence.

We're not the only ones who come here ya know.

Jade Who else?

Jordan That girl from school.

Jade Yeah which one?

Jordan Reffo.

Jade Ishtar?

Jordan Yeah.
Her and some surfie.

Jade What Finn?

Jordan Ya know him?

Jade Yeah Finn's cool.
Jordan Saw 'em
  like together 'n' that.
Jade Pervert.
Jordan Wha'?
Jade Watched 'em at it did ya?
Jordan Jus' saw 'em go in here didn't follow 'em.
Jade Yeah righto.
  Reckon they're doin' it?
Jordan What do you reckon?

  Silence.

Jade Imagine hundreds of years ago
  seein' them white people comin' round the headlands in
  their ships?
Jordan You'd shit yerself.

  Silence.

Jade So what's with the look?

  JORDAN gets up, collects her stuff.

  I mean are you a guy or a chick?
  Or don't you know yet?

  JORDAN leaves the cave.

  Hey.

SCENE

The school toilets.

Rick C Block dunnies.
Jade Next day at school.
Lara Jade run so much she out of fuel.
Rick So we're waggin' class.
Lara Got PE
Rick then double history.
All Pass.
Rick I'm bored.
  Sittin' in me bedroom pickin' me bellybutton fluff
  be more buzzin' than this.

ISHTAR enters.

She doesn't see the others, goes to a cubicle and throws up.

The girls sit up, listen and watch.

ISHTAR exits the cubicle, washes her face and then looks in the mirror.

She takes out the hijab stuffed in her backpack and puts it on.

LARA drapes a cloth over her head like a mock hijab and creeps up on ISHTAR.

Lara Hey Ishtar?

ISHTAR starts.

Scare ya?

Think I was ya freaky mother?

ISHTAR tries to leave but LARA blocks her.

Don't think you should be allowed to wear that.

It's not school uniform.

Jade Lara.

Lara What?

Just sayin' what everyone's thinkin'.

Got a right to free speech.

It's a free country.

Ishtar Yeah?

Well you're racist and it's ugly.

Lara You're racist look at ya.

You're racist against Aussies.

Anyway what you wearin' that for all of a sudden?

Ya never used to.

It suddenly come into fashion?

Ishtar You should try it cover up your crap haircut.

Lara Watch yourself mut.

What are you doin' with our Finn?

We all seen ya holdin' hands 'n' pashin'.

You sleepin' with him?

He's one of us

so get ya hands off him.

Ishtar You're just jealous

'cos you're still a virgin.

LARA thrusts her lighter at ISHTAR's hijab.

Jade Hey.
   Hey.
Lara Only doin' what her own peeps do.
   Don't they burn skanks like you?

   JADE intervenes.

   The screech of a loudspeaker.

   Reckon you should get rid of that if ya know what's good for ya.
Rick Loudspeaker screams and creams our ears.
Jade It's Miss Dimple
   the school principal
   announcing an
Teacher all-grades emergency parade.
Lara We drag our feet.
Rick Mrs Brooke shooin' us like chooks.
Teacher Hurry up girls hurry up
Rick she clucks.
Jade We take our sweet time.
   Stuff the old duck.
Lara Look there's cops.
Rick I'm off.
Jade Stop.
Rick Why not?
Jade 'Cos you'll look all guilty.
Rick I can't get busted no way me dad'll kill me.
Jade Just chill.
Rick He will.
Jade Take a pill.
   They don't know it was us.
   Trus' me.
Lara So principal goes off with
   blahdy blah blah
   goes rahdy rah rah.
Rick Spittin' gibberish through her fat lips.
Jade She lets rip
   about the break-in at the primary school
   about
Teacher senseless destruction

23

Jade and

Teacher deviant behaviour.

Lara We're like

All oohhh ah mah.

Jade She goes ballistic
　　calls us

Teacher delinquent.

Jade Yardy-ya whatever.

Lara Truth is

Rick we're pissin' our pants
　　'cos there be a chance
　　cops know who we are.

Lara But Jade's cool
　　goes

Jade no way nah.

Rick So we relax
　　sit back.

Lara Flick the switch to nap phase
　　our eyes glaze
　　few z's later…

All Snap.

Rick She still on about how we got

Teacher no respect.

Lara Ain't this lecture ended yet?

Jade Give it a rest.

　　　The girls depart.

　　　JADE and ISHTAR remain.

　　Hey.
　　Hey Ishtar?

Ishtar What?

Jade Why'd you start wearin' that?

　　　JADE refers to ISHTAR's hijab.

Ishtar 'Cos of all your Aussie shit.

Jade Sorry hey.
　　'Bout what happened in the toilet and that.

Ishtar Reckon I won't fight back?

SCENE

JADE is running.

A fragmented radio news report.

Voice Cummergunja Abattoir… yesterday… suspending operation… further notice… possible closure… leaving one hundred and eighty workers…

> *JADE arrives at the cave breathless, rips out her earphones.*

Jade Hey.

> *JORDAN doesn't respond.*

Brought some stuff for ya.

> *She tosses the stuff inside the cave.*

> *Silence.*

Jus' biscuits and a blanket.

Jordan Am I ya stray dog now?

Jade What?

Jordan Ya after-school project?

Jade Nuh.

Jordan Where's ya gang?
Why aren't ya hangin' with 'em?

Jade Take the shit back then.

Jordan Nah leave it.

> *Silence.*

> *JADE begins to leave.*

Saw 'em again.

Jade Who?

Jordan Them two.
They come here the other day.

Jade Ishtar and Finn?

Jordan Yeah.

Jade You seen Ishtar's mum?

Jordan Yeah weird aye?

Jade Looks sad I reckon.

Jordan Why she meetin' him here?
Aren't them girls allowed to have boyfriends?

Jade Dunno.

Not surfies anyways.

Finn's alright but don't reckon his dreads gunna impress her.

Jordan They probably stone her if they knew hey?

Jade What?

Jordan I dunno that's what they do.

Jade Who?

Jordan Them reffos.

Jade Who said that?

Jordan Jus' heard it somewhere.

Silence.

Jade Shouldn't call 'em that.

Jordan Your mates do.

Silence.

Jade You sleep here every night?

Jordan Whenever.

Jade Got a foster family don't ya?

Don't you like 'em?

Silence.

My mum's not home much.

I'm gone runnin' she don't even notice.

I could be dead

hit by a truck.

Silence.

What about your mum?

JORDAN shrugs.

Don't ya know who she is?

Jordan Nuh

Jade S'cool.

Jordan Wha'?

Jade Yeah 'cos you could be anyone couldn't ya?

Your mum could be like rich or famous.

Rest of us all know who we are where we're from.

Jordan Make me sound all special or somethin'.

Jade We're headin' out tonight.

Wanna come?

Jordan Where to?

Jade Dunno club somewhere.

Jordan With all youse?

Jade Whole pack of us.

Jordan Nuh.

Jade They're all cool
known 'em since school.
Known Lara since I was born.
Done all sorts of stuff together us.

Jordan Yeah like play Barbies?

Jade Piss off.

    Silence.

Ya know that break-in at the school?
How that classroom got trashed?
That was us.

    JORDAN throws JADE an unimpressed look.

    JORDAN gathers up her stuff.

Ya comin' out with us or not?

    JORDAN walks away.

I got some stuff.

    JORDAN stops.

Jordan Yeah?

SCENE

The park.

LARA and RICK are hanging out.

JADE appears with JORDAN.

Lara Who's that?

Jade She's cool trus' me.

Lara She stabbed that girl through the hand with a pencil.

Rick Is she actually a chick?

Lara You've really flipped
you've tripped Jade.
You've knocked your head on a rock.
What is up with you?

Jade We're sisters aren't we?

Lara Maybe.

Jade Stronger than blood us.
Lara S'pose.
Jade Then trus' me.
Lara Yeah okay but this is crap.
Jade Hey Jordan get here
    meet the rest of the pack.

    Silence.

Rick So where to?
Jade RSL.
Rick Yeah your mum'll be there Lara
    she'll sign us all in.
Lara Nuh she won't be.
Rick Yeah she's always there playin' the pokies
    twenty-four seven.
Lara Say it again I'll smash ya face in.
Rick Jus' jokin'.
Lara Anyway don't wanna go.
    RSL's slow
    only play golden oldies.
Jade So we'll have 'em dancin' to Pink
    sing some karaoke.

SCENE

The Cummergunja RSL Club.

Jade So we rock up the RSL
    wanna run amuck.
    Climate like the Ice Age so we crank it up.
Lara See RSL's where all the teachers unwind
Rick get blind.
Lara Dancin' like this
Rick feelin' each other up.
Lara/Rick/Jade It's sick.
Lara Oh my god don't look now it's too fugly.
    There be Miss Cutcliff
    dancin' dirty with Mr Rugby.
Jade She still baldy?
    Wearin' her wig is she?
Rick She's all unsteady.

Lara He's proppin' her up.

Jade/Lara/Rick She is totally cactus.

Rick In the pokies room
    there's Lara's mum.
    She goes

Lara's Mum Free spins are up darlin'
    get me another one.

Jade Lara's had it but.

Lara Jus' go home Mum.

Lara's Mum I'm havin' fun.
    Never asked youse to come.

Lara Didn't ya get a shift?

Lara's Mum Nup
    got the flick
    but guess how much I've won?

Lara None?

Lara's Mum Bunch a cows
    you and ya friends.
    I buy youse drinks
    sign youse in.

    The RSL minute of silence siren sounds.

    Shush.
    Show some respect and stand up.

Lara Get stuffed.

Rick Then Jade runs biff
    into Miss Cutcliff.

Miss Cutliff Jade.

Jade Miss.

Miss Cutliff So good to see you Jade.
    You promised to come back to school and visit me.
    I suppose you're busy.
    How's your poetry?
    Published yet?

Jade Poetry's gay miss.

Miss Cutliff I'm sorry to hear that.
    You had a gift.

Jade Why do you say that
    when you know it's bullshit?

Miss Cutliff Is everything okay Jade?

29

Jade I'm fine.

You're the one pissed miss.

Miss Cutliff This isn't like you.

Jade What would you know?

Hey Jordan let's go.

Miss Cutliff Jade.

Jade Don't touch me.

Lara Rest of us chicks still muckin' up.

Cut in on the oldies on the dance floor.

Show 'em some new moves they never seen before.

Rick Here look Granny

this is how ya do the doggy.

Lara Who are you callin' dirty?

Rick Stuck-up farts.

Lara Dried-up tarts.

Rick Ya reckon they ever have sex?

Lara Nuh no way.

Rick Yeah they got broken parts.

Rick/Lara They shuffle back to their tables

practically disabled.

The music stops.

Lara Then the music stops.

The mood drops.

Rick What the hell?

Lara Still we keep dancin'.

Rick They can't stop us.

Lara We're still spinnin'

we're still buzzin' to the booze

cruisin' through our blood stream.

Lara Then we look over and we see this scene.

Lara/Rick It's Jade and Jordan pashin'

Lara and I'm sick all of a sudden.

Rick They are kissin' full on the lips

tongue mouth teeth and spit.

Goes on forever doesn't it?

Lara Think I'm gunna vomit.

Rick Then the manager

all gravy-stained and fattest loser

grabs 'em and drags 'em both out the back.
Blue-rinsers staring death rays through their cataracts.

> *The MANAGER grabs JADE and JORDAN and hauls them outside.*

Jade Let go fatso.

Manager What do you think you're playin' at?

Jade Just dancin' that's all.

Manager You're spoiling everyone's evening with your hijinks.

Jade Just havin' some fun.

Manager This is a licensed venue and you're both underage.

Jade You let us in
  served us drinks.

Manager I've called the police.

Jade We're goin'.

Manager No you're not.

Jordan Don't touch her.

Manager You shut up.

Jordan Let us go or I'll tell the pigs you felt us up.

Manager You what?

Jordan You heard it.

Manager Wait a minute.

Jade Both of us will.

Manager You little…
  I haven't touched you.

Jordan We'll tell the cops you fingered us.

Manager Piss off and don't come back.

> *JADE and JORDAN bolt from the MANAGER and run into LARA
> and RICK.*

Lara You a lesbo now
  Jade that it?

Jade Nuh.

Lara Then what's with the tongue gym
  on the dance floor just then?

Jade Don't crack.
  Just stirrin' up
  givin' the old farts a heart attack.
  Isn't that right Jord?

> *Pause.*

Hey?
Got a problem with that?
Lara?

Lara Nuh.
Got a problem with your stray dog but.

> *JORDAN launches herself at LARA, JADE holds JORDAN back.*

Here boy here boy sic.
I'd watch her Jade
reckon she's got AIDS.

Jade Just piss off.

Lara Was gunna.
Come on Rick.

> *RICK checks with JADE.*

> *JADE shakes her off.*

Jade Go.

> *LARA and RICK leave.*

I'm still buzzin'.

Jordan Yeah.

Jade Let's do somethin'
let's run.

SCENE

Night.

The sound of glass breaking and shouting.

A car hoons up the street.

The sound of women wailing fades into waves crashing on the beach.

SCENE

The cave.

Jade That was shit back there
what Lara said to ya.
I was just muckin' up.

> *Pause.*

You're not freakin' out are ya?

Jordan Nuh.

Jade Won't do it again.

Jordan Try 'n' I'll stab ya.

Silence.

Jade Feel like I sorta know ya.

Jordan Yeah?

Jade Like I've known ya before.

Jordan Yeah?

Pause.

Like when?

Jade Another life maybe.
You believe in that?
Maybe like in this cave.
Like you 'n' me used to hang out.
Maybe this was our home
hundreds of years ago.

Jordan Yeah?

Jade Hey ever seen cave paintings
ones the Aboriginals did?
None round here.
Wish there was.
Handprints.
Sort of a sign from them that they was here
owned this place.
Hey come and live at my house.

Jordan Wha'?

Jade Can't keep sleepin' here.
I'll tell my mum.
We can be sisters.

Jordan Sisters?

Jade Whatever.
We can share my room.
Stuff Lara.
Wanna?

Jordan Yeah righto.

Silence.

Jade You ever kissed anyone?

Jordan Yeah.

Jade Yeah?

> *Pause.*

Do ya like guys or chicks?

> *Pause.*

Come on won't tell anyone.
Guys or chicks?

> *Pause.*

Jordan Chicks
guess.

Jade What?
Didn't hear ya.

Jordan Chicks.

> *JADE grabs JORDAN.*

> *They kiss, then JADE breaks away.*

Jade Know how sometimes shit gets in?
Gets in ya head 'n' ya can't get rid of it?

Jordan Yeah.

Jade I try 'n' run it out but it won't go.
Can't run fast enough.
Can't run hard enough.

Jordan Raped ya didn't they?
Was up here that night.
Then saw ya on the beach.
Raped ya didn't they?

Jade Met 'em at the club.
Was dancin' with 'em.
They were buyin' me drinks.
Asked me down the beach.
Went with 'em.
Dumb stupid slut
went with 'em.

Jordan Never said yes.

Jade Nuh.

Jordan Raped ya.

Jade Thought I could handle 'em.
Tell anyone I'll kill ya.

JADE grabs her stuff, heads out of the cave.

Jordan What's up?
Jade Gotta run.

JADE runs from the cave.

SCENE

School grounds.

ISHTAR charges up to JADE, shoves her.

WOMEN in hijab appear.

They travel slowly as if on a long journey. One falls and the others continue on.

Ishtar Why are you doing this to us?
Jade Hey?

ISHTAR shoves JADE again.

Ishtar Why?
Jade What?
Ishtar You know what.
Jade No.
Ishtar The pig's head through our window last night.
Jade Wasn't me. Wasn't us.
Ishtar Yeah right.
Jade Wasn't. I swear.
Ishtar They're all your mates.
Jade Could've been anyone in town.
Ishtar Anyone?
Jade With Damo dead.
Ishtar That's got nothin' to do with us.
Jade The meatworks closin'.
Ishtar Or that.
Jade Still.
Ishtar Still what?

Pause.

Jade I dunno.
Everyone's lost their job you know.
Everyone's pissed off.

Ishtar That's not our fault.
    That's not about us.
Jade Youse are alright aren't ya?
Ishtar No we're not.
    My mum thinks soldiers are coming for us.
    She won't let us call the police.
    She can't sleep.
    None of you know anything about us.

    Silence.

Jade Yeah well we had nothing to do with it.
Ishtar You think you're different
    but you're just like the rest of them.

    ISHTAR leaves.

    The sound of women wailing.

SCENE

The school.

Lara Sorry.

    JADE says nothing.

    Said I'm sorry.
Jade Yeah?
Lara Well?
Jade What?
Lara Said I'm sorry.
Jade Heard ya.
Lara Waitin'.
Jade For what?
Lara Somethin' back.
Jade What?
Lara You tell me.
Jade S'posed to say I'm sorry too?
Lara Yeah.
Jade It's you should be sorryin' me.
Lara I was I am I said it.
Jade Ya shouldn't have said that stuff.
    Ya lucky I never mashed ya.
Lara You mash a sister?

Jade Just warnin' ya.

Lara Shouldn't have said that.

Okay?

Still me sister aren't ya?

Jade Yeah.

Lara Since preschool

since before then

since we was born.

Jade/Lara Since we was sperm.

Lara I was a total bitch.

Jade So was I.

Lara Least we're both hot.

Jade True.

Missed you.

Lara Ya have gone lesbo haven't ya?

Jade Piss off.

Lara You comin' to the park tonight or what?

Jade Dunno.

Lara It's a long weekender

ANZAC bender.

Jade diggers died for this

ya can't miss it.

There's gunna be a big bonfire in honour of Damo.

We're gunna sing a song.

It'll go off.

Promise.

>   *Pause.*

Ya know that pig's head got chucked through the reffo's window last night?

Jade Yeah.

Lara That was us.

Ricky 'n' me gave the Kings a ring after youse left.

Went draggin'.

Total crack-up.

See Jade ya not the only one who can muck up.

>   *JADE is silent.*

So ya'll be there Jade won't ya?

Jade Yeah.

JADE walks away.

Lara And don't BYO freak okay?
It's jus' the pack.

LARA is gone.

Jade No.

SCENE

LARA to audience.

Lara So it was a long weekender
ANZAC bender.

Rick Diggers died for this.

Lara So we're hangin' in the Memorial Park after dark.
We give the Kings a ring

Rick 'cos we're gunna get wasted
we're gunna get pasted.

Lara And we're gunna sing a song for Damo.

Rick Yeah 'cos he's like everyone's hero.

Lara Then Jade rocks up
with her mongrel stray
ruins everythin'.

The scene morphs into the Memorial Park.

Rick Here comes the queen bee

Lara finally.

Rick Who she with?

Lara How come 'its' here?

Jade She's with me.

Lara This party is private.
'It' ain't invited.

Jade This park yours now is it?
You own it?

Lara Yeah.

Jade Get over it.

Rick Then you see Lara rearin' up
suckin' the air 'n' gearin' up.

Lara You used to be hot Jade you usta be one of us
now look at ya.

Rick We looked up to ya.

Lara You usta be the style queen now ya got some disease
   wearin' army fatigues.
   Why you hangin' out with that psycho all of a sudden?
   You don't belong with her.
Rick You belong with us.
Lara And why you got this thing with chicks?
   Everyone knows you blew those four dudes at the club.
Rick Did she do 'em?
Jordan Did not.
Jade Shut up.
Lara What?
Jordan They raped her
   down the beach.

   Silence.

Lara Bull
   shit.
Rick That true Jade?
   Huh?
Lara Bull
   shit.
Jordan True.
Lara How come you tellin' 'it' and not us?
Rick Aren't us good enough?
Lara What ya got to say for yerself Jade?
   Huh?

   JADE talks straight to JORDAN.

Jade I did 'em.
   All four of 'em at once.
   Loved it.
   I took 'em all on.

   LARA to JORDAN.

Lara See
   it's bullshit.
   Knew it.
   Truth is freak
   Jade's
   a
   slut.

39

JORDAN flares up ready to attack.

Jade [*to JORDAN*] Piss off.
  Said
  piss
  off.
  [*To LARA*] We're done.

> *LARA climbs on the statue.*

Lara Look at me I'm Jade
  down the beach.
  Gunna do these soldiers
  'cos I'm a/slut.

Rick Then Jade flipped
  lost it proper.

> *LARA and JADE fight.*

  Thought she was gunna mash ya Lara.
  Then...

> *RICK looks over at the statue.*

> *ISHTAR is there with a spray can, painting it.*

  What the hell?
  Ishtar's graffin' up the statue.
  'ANZAC murderers
  War is Rape'.
  Hey.

> *ISHTAR takes off, the girls pursue her.*

Lara/Rick Hey.

> *Sirens.*

Ishtar Shit.

All Cops.

> *The girls run.*

> *The girls halt, they've been cornered by the cops.*

Lara They pick us all up on the highway.
  Figured we was the ones
  'cos we got white paint on us
  but we wasn't.

> *Darkness.*

A police prison cell.
MEN appear and encircle JADE.

Jade Hey.
    I did it.
    Jus' me.
    Let 'em go.
    They never touched the statue.
    I graff'd it up.
    Trashed the primary school too.
    So hurry up and charge me.
    Said hurry up and charge me pigs.
    Don't fuckin' touch me
    don't fuckin' touch me
    don't.

      Darkness.

SCENE

Lara So anyway this is crap
    Jade owned up
    she took the rap.
Rick So lucky
    me dad would've killed me.
    He was in Vietnam
    and once on Anzac Day
    he got so drunk
    he pissed in the hallway.
Lara Don't share
    Rick no-one cares.

      She turns to ISHTAR.

    Do ya wanna speak freak?
    Cough up gob up
    come on spit.
Ishtar I did it.
Lara No shit.
    Yeah but funniest bit

was when Finn found out
you was pregnant
he dropped ya terrorist arse on the grass fast.
Knew youse wouldn't last.

Rick Then the meatworks shut down.

Lara Yeah shut down the whole town.

Rick 'Memba that school excursion to the abattoir?

Lara Stunk o' murder.

Rick Someone's mum in a shower cap
covered in blood and guts
givin' us a lecture.

Lara I ain't workin' there ever.

Rick Me neither.

Lara I'd rather be a bludger.
So everyone in town
is in line at Centrelink
jus' hangin' round.

Rick Ripped off.

Lara Pissed off.

Rick That's when things took off.

Lara Someone sends round a texty.

Rick I didn't get it 'cos I ain't got no moby.

Lara Get down the Memorial Park tomorrow and show your
respects.

Rick Damo died for us.

Lara Go home reffo terrorists.

SCENE

Sunday.

It's dawn on ANZAC Day.

*Fragments of radio talkback and news reports. A rally is building at the
Memorial Park in town.*

JADE runs.

Jade Four a.m. runnin' again
circling the town
eyes to ground
joints locked

runners pounding black rock
gun it up the big hill
road kill chewing gum can of Bundy rum
sweat drips road eats it
bite down on lip
grip slips
trip
knee first
bitumen rips
blood drips
don't quit.

Men Ute get in it.

Jade Wanna go home now.

Men You asked for it.

Jade Leg it.

Men Now beg for it.

Jade Sting kicks in
bare teeth 'n' grin it.

Men You want it.

Jade Gun it.

Men Say it.

Jade Gear up 'n' bolt

Men You love it.

Jade Reach the peak 'n' fault
grind to a halt.

> *JADE stops when she sees SAMIRA standing in the middle of the road.*
>
> *SAMIRA is disorientated and, in her mind, she is back in Iraq fleeing through the mountains.*
>
> *Two WOMEN, also in hijab, follow her, unseen by JADE.*

Samira [*in Arabic*] They are coming for us
sleep with one eye open
a knife under the bed
a suitcase packed.
They will come from the ends of the earth.
They are coming.
They are coming.

Jade Hey.

Hey.

SAMIRA sees JADE and is frightened.

You're in the middle of the road.
You'll get hit by a car.
What are you doing out here?

She shows JADE a picture of her daughter, ISHTAR.

Ishtar?

Samira Your friend?

Jade I go to school with her.

Samira Have you seen her?

Jade No
    not since…

Samira When?

Jade Friday night.

Samira Where did you see her?

Jade At the Memorial Park.
    The Memorial Park in town.

Samira She did not come home last night.

Jade She could be with Finn.

Samira Finn?
    Who is Finn?

Jade You been down the beach?
    Checked up the caves?

Samira I look everywhere.

Jade I dunno where she is.

Samira They have taken her.

Jade Who?

Samira They have come.
    The men the soldiers.
    They have taken her.
    They have taken my daughter.

Jade You should go home.
    Maybe she's there.
    It's not safe in town right now.
    You should go home.

SAMIRA is gone.

44

SCENE

JADE runs to the cave.

JADE sees aerosol painted handprints covering the cave walls.

JORDAN appears from inside the cave.

Jade What's this?

Jordan It's like them paintings you talked about
like them handprints the Kooris did.

> *Pause.*

Copied 'em from pictures.
Found this book in the library at school.
Tried to get all the colours right.
Ya know how you reckon we could've lived here?
You 'n' me in this cave?
Reckon that's true ya know.
Reckon this was home.
Reckon I'm gunna go lookin' for me mum.
Ya wanna come?

Jade Why'd you do this?

Jordan Say sorry
sorry for rattin' on ya.

Jade Trusted ya.

Jordan They called you a slut.

Jade So what?

Jordan You're not.

Jade What would you know?

> *Silence.*

Jordan Won't let 'em say that stuff about ya.

Jade Should've kept ya mouth shut.

Jordan Sorry Jade sorry.
Jus' anyone ever touches ya
anyone ever hurts ya.

Jade What?

Jordan I'd do 'em Jade.
I'd kill 'em.

> *Pause.*

Jade Yer off ya face.

Jordan Nuh I'm not.
Jade Shouldn't have done this
shouldn't have touched this place.
It's sacred.
Told ya.
Jordan I'll fix it Jade.
I'll scrub it off.
Jade This is shit.
Jordan Thought ya'd like it.
Jordan Jade.

She tries to touch JADE.

JADE shrinks away.

JORDAN lashes out.

She shoves JADE violently against the wall.
Scared I'm gunna stab ya?
Are ya?
Are ya?

She retreats into the dark.
You don't know what's in me.

JORDAN runs off.

ISHTAR arrives, carrying a backpack.

Jade Are you lookin' for Finn?
Ishtar Have you seen him?
Jade No.

ISHTAR heads off.
Saw ya mum up on the road but.
She's lookin' for ya.

ISHTAR loses it, throws her bag, breaks down.

Silence.
Why'd you graff up the statue?
Ishtar 'Cos I felt like it.
Jade More than that.
Ishtar 'Cos I'm angry.
Aren't you?
Jade What's wrong with your mum?

Ishtar Stuff happened to her back in Iraq.

Jade What stuff?

Ishtar She won't tell me.
  Whatever it is she can't get rid of it.
  She's got all this shit in her head.

    Pause.

  You don't know what it's like to have to run
  spend years in a refugee camp
  lose everything.
  She did all that for me.
  Now I've shamed her.

Jade What 'cos of the statue?
  I took the rap.
  She doesn't have to know.

Ishtar I'm pregnant.
  And now Finn's pissed off.

Jade Probably just freakin' out.
  He'll come back.

Ishtar Yeah?

Jade Yeah Finn's alright.

    ISHTAR notices the handprints on the cave walls.

    She places her hand on one of the prints.

Ishtar Who did this?
  It's amazing.

    JADE looks again at the prints.

    ISHTAR grabs her bag and heads out of the cave.

Jade Ishtar ya better find her.
  She seems really messed up.

Ishtar Where is she?

Jade She's gone back to town I think.
   Maybe the Memorial Park
  I dunno.

    ISHTAR leaves.

    JADE remains, looking up at the handprints.

    A hum.

    JADE bolts from the cave.

There is a crowd at the Memorial Park.

SAMIRA appears, carrying a can of petrol.

Samira Where have you taken her?
I want my daughter.

The town begins to merge into a war zone.

Where have you taken her?
Please give me my daughter.

SAMIRA drenches herself with petrol from the can.

Darkness.

A hum.

JORDAN is spraying her body with ochre-coloured aerosol.

She inhales the paint.

JADE is running.

Jade Wake up
back seat
vinyl sticks to cheek
alchie breath
feel sick
taste sweat
waves pound the beach
dry reach.

Four MEN converge on JADE, pulling, pushing, shoving, groping, ripping.

Men She awake?
Jade Please I wanna go home.
Men Not yet.
Jade No.
Men Come here.
Jade That hurts.
Men You asked for it.
Jade Please.
Men Beg for it.
Jade Let me go.
Men You wanted it.
Say it.
Jade No.

Stop
stop
stop
stop.

Men Durry break.

Jade Wait.
Durry fireflies do tricks
count cigarettes one two three four
hand grips door
push
slip through it
run for it
trip
split lip
get up quick.

Men Come back ya fuckin' bitch.

Jade Bolt
hit the edge of the cliff

She leaps into the air.

vault

She is falling.

wait to smash up
mash up
eyes shut.

Out of the dark comes JORDAN, painted up.

Out of the dark comes JADE, running.

Out of the dark comes SAMIRA, drenched in petrol, calling out in anguished Arabic.

Samira Where is my daughter?!
Where have you taken her?!
Where is my daughter?!
Where is God?!
Where is God?!

She tears off her hijab.

She holds out a cigarette lighter.

ISHTAR embraces SAMIRA, wrapping her in the hijab.

49

ISHTAR speaks in Arabic.

Ishtar No Oummi!

    She takes the lighter from SAMIRA.

We're safe now.
No-one's coming for us.
We're safe here.

    In English now.

We're safe now.
No-one's coming for us.
We're safe here.

    ISHTAR and SAMIRA disappear into darkness.
    JADE leaps from the cliff, falls into darkness.
    JORDAN disappears into darkness.
    Waves crashing on the beach.
    JADE wakes, looks around, no-one is there.

SCENE

LARA, JADE, RICK and ISHTAR appear.

Lara Yeah so that's the story.
Rest is history.

    The light slowly fades out over the following scene which ends in darkness.

Rick What we gunna do now
we got expelled from school?

Lara Plenty of shit
hey Rick?

Rick What?

Lara Not worried us.
There's always...

Rick Huh?

Lara Think.

Rick/Lara Centrelink.

Rick Maybe we should've tried to stay
like Jade.
Gone to night school

that be pretty cool.
Jade what ya gunna do at the end of the year?

Jade Leave here.
Go to the city
study maybe.

Rick What?

Jade Dunno
could do teaching.

Lara Boring.

Jade Reckon?
You've never even been to the city.

Lara Nothin' there you can't get here.
We got Macca's Red Rooter Kentucky.

Jade Yeah aren't we lucky?

Ishtar World doesn't end here you know.
There's places out there.

Jade Yeah.

Lara So?

Rick We'll never get to go.
Hey Jade can I come visit ya?

Jade Maybe.

Lara Ya wouldn't last a day in the city
Ricky.

Jade We'll see. What you gunna do Ishtar?

Ishtar Finish school
raise my daughter
Samira.

Ishtar Hey Jade?

Jade Yeah?

Ishtar Where'd that girl Jordan go?

Jade She jus' took off
hitchhiked
disappeared
I dunno.

   Pause.

Maybe she went home.

   LARA yawns.

Lara Come on Rick let's split.

JADE loses it, coming after LARA as she's leaving.

RICK steps between them.

Rick Jade
leave it.
Leave it Jade.

JADE backs off.

Lara What?
What'd I do?
Crazy bitch.

RICK turns to LARA.

Rick Shut up.

JADE walks away.

Hey Jade?
What's this town mean again?
The name?

Jade/Ishtar Home.

SCENE

The cave.

A hum.

Darkness.

JADE spray-paints the walls of the cave.

Morning light.

Waves on the beach.

Jade Wherever you are Jordan
you'll never be forgotten.

THE END